20 OF THEIR BEST ARRANGED BY PHILLIP KEVEREN

— PIANO LEVEL —
INTERMEDIATE

ISBN 978-1-5400-3272-0

Hal•Leonard®

Visit Hal Leonard Online at
www.halleonard.com

Visit Phillip at
www.phillipkeveren.com

Contact us:
Hal Leonard
7777 West Bluemound Road
Milwaukee, WI 53213
Email: info@halleonard.com

In Europe, contact:
Hal Leonard Europe Limited
Distribution Centre, Newmarket Road
Bury St Edmunds, Suffolk, IP33 3YB
Email: info@halleonardeurope.com

In Australia, contact:
Hal Leonard Australia Pty. Ltd.
4 Lentara Court
Cheltenham, Victoria, 3192 Australia
Email: info@halleonard.com.au

BIOGRAPHY

Phillip Keveren, a multi-talented keyboard artist and composer, has composed original works in a variety of genres from piano solo to symphonic orchestra. He gives frequent concerts and workshops for teachers and their students in the United States, Canada, Europe, Australia, and Asia. Mr. Keveren holds a B.M. in composition from California State University Northridge and a M.M. in composition from the University of Southern California.

PREFACE

I turned nine years old in the summer of 1970. It was a typically boiling hot eastern Oregon summer, and the community swimming pool was not just entertainment. It was literally survival in an era before most folks had air conditioning. When I first heard "Close to You" drifting out of the pool's radio speakers, I was pretty certain that Karen was singing just for me, so immediate and intimate was her vocal reading. Richard's arrangement and keyboard licks appealed to my just developing piano skills. Thus began my lifelong love of Carpenters music.

Fast forward to the summer of 1980. I was a participant in an electronic organ festival sponsored by Yamaha in those days. I advanced to the national finals, held at the University of Southern California in Los Angeles. Richard Carpenter was on the judging panel, and Karen came along to listen to the concert. Having the opportunity to visit with the two of them after the event was the highlight of the entire festival for me. Their encouragement inspired me to keep studying and refining my musical craft. It also taught me how a few kind words can make all the difference to young musicians I meet in my professional engagements.

Choosing which songs to feature in this book was not an easy task. The biggest hits are more obvious, but there are dozens of deep catalogue songs that could have joined the collection. Some arrangements are based closely on the original Carpenters recordings ("Close to You," "Yesterday Once More"), while others are fresh pianistic interpretations. "Top of the World" has a playful classical flavor, and "Please Mr. Postman" is more Mozart than Motown. All were crafted with a deep and abiding love for the music Richard and Karen Carpenter gave the world.

Sincerely,

Phillip Keveren

L-R: Karen Carpenter, 19-year-old Phillip Keveren, Mariya Kawashima, Richard Carpenter.

CONTENTS

BECAUSE WE ARE IN LOVE
(The Wedding Song)

Words and Music by RICHARD CARPENTER
and JOHN BETTIS
Arranged by Phillip Keveren

Expressively, with rubato ♩ = c. 96

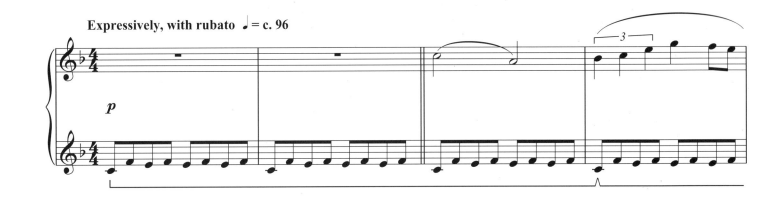

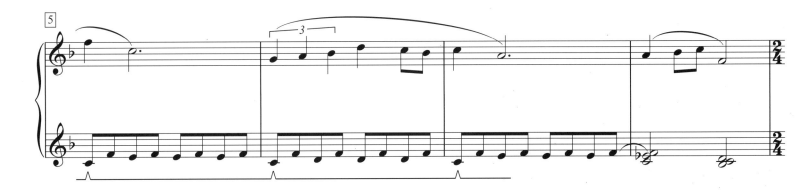

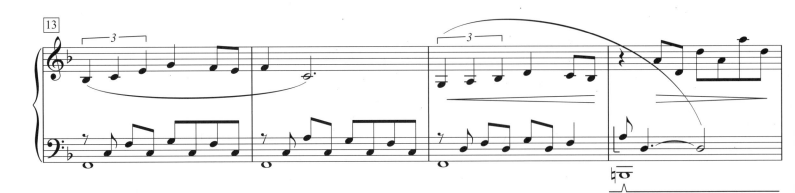

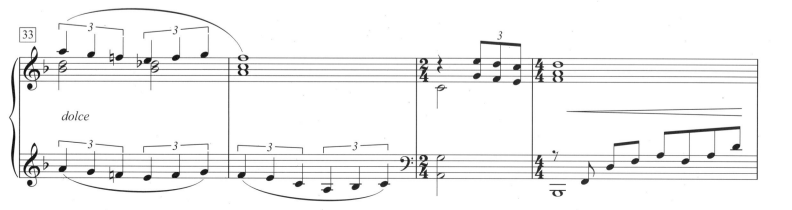

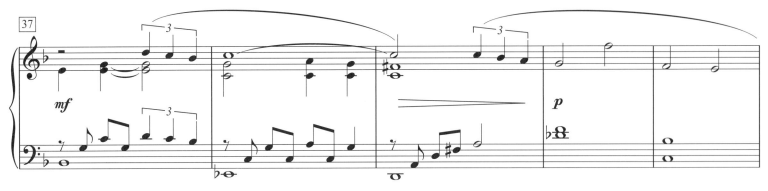

Flowing ♩ = c. 104

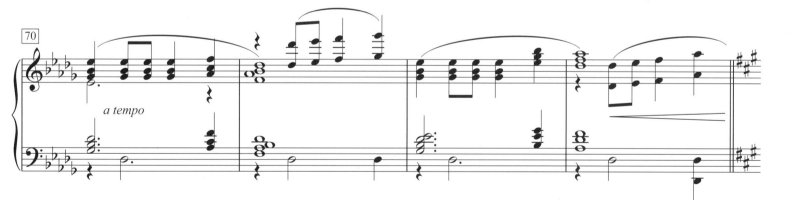

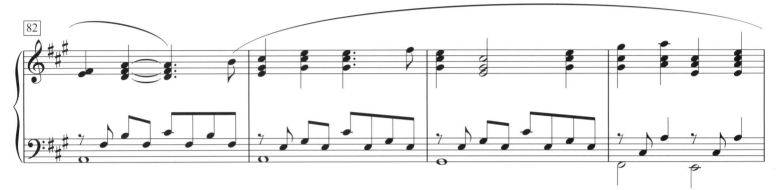

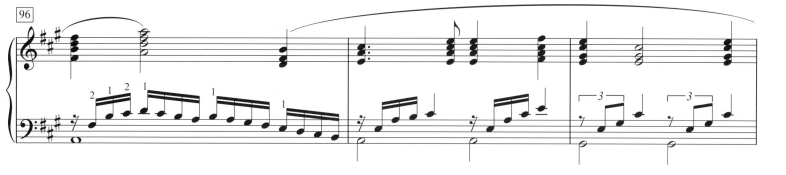

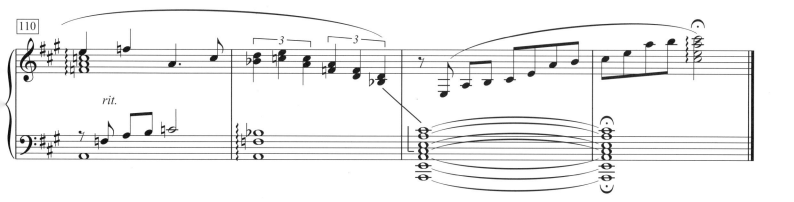

BLESS THE BEASTS AND THE CHILDREN

Words and Music by BARRY DeVORZON
and PERRY BOTKIN, JR.
Arranged by Phillip Keveren

Tenderly ♩ = 80

With pedal

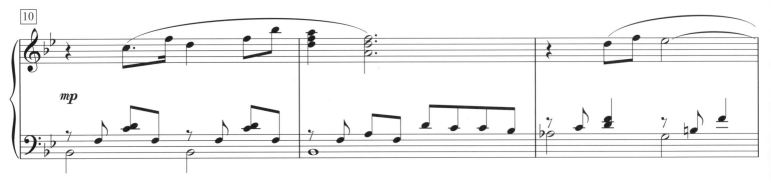

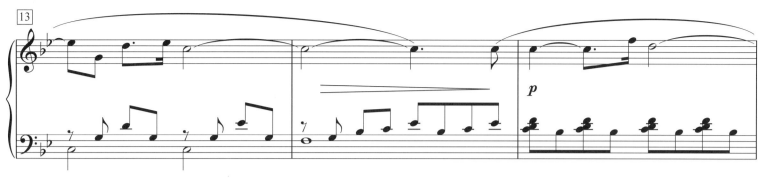

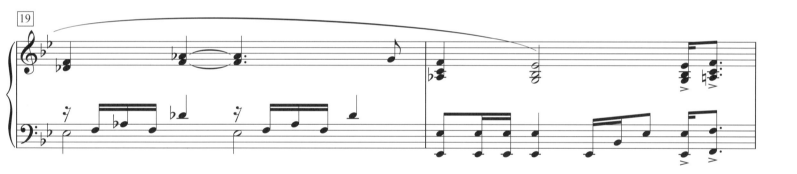

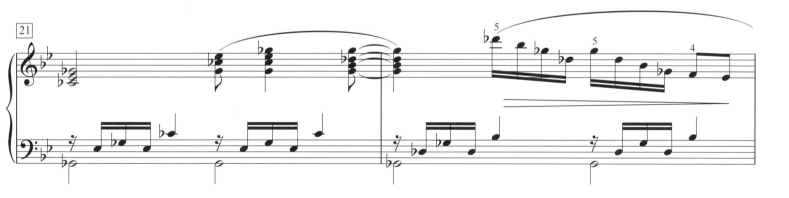

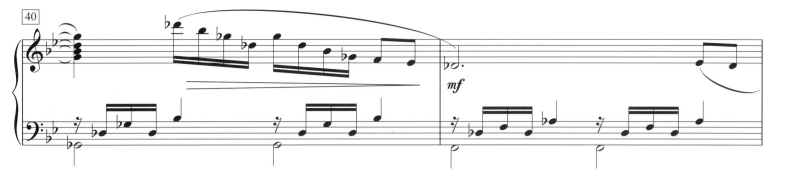

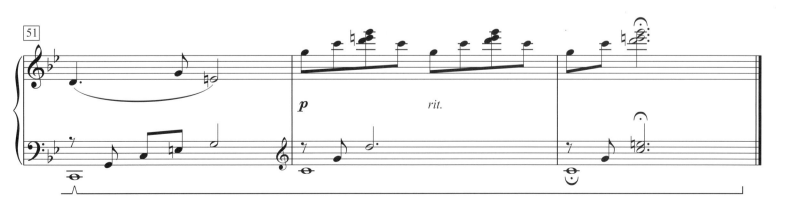

(They Long to Be)
CLOSE TO YOU

Lyrics by HAL DAVID
Music by BURT BACHARACH
Arranged by Phillip Keveren

Relaxed ♩ = 88

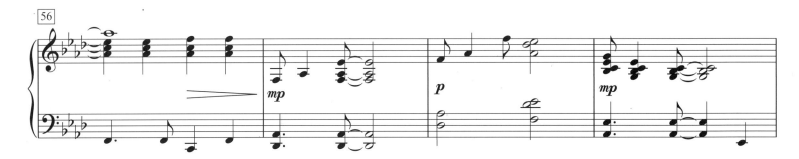

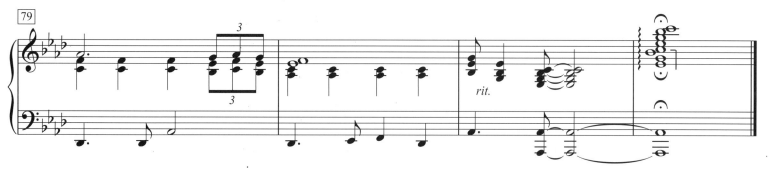

FOR ALL WE KNOW

from the Motion Picture LOVERS AND OTHER STRANGERS

Words by ROBB WILSON
and ARTHUR JAMES
Music by FRED KARLIN
Arranged by Phillip Keveren

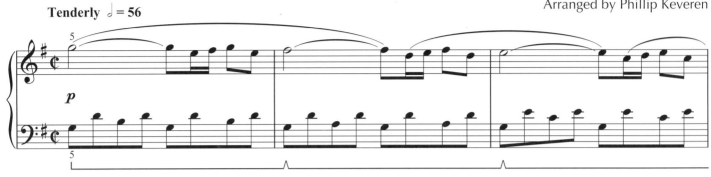

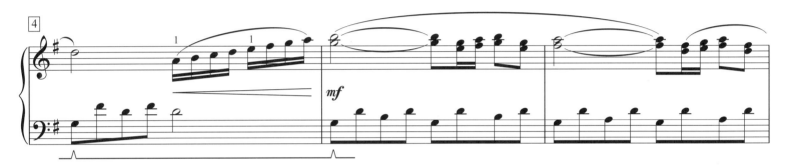

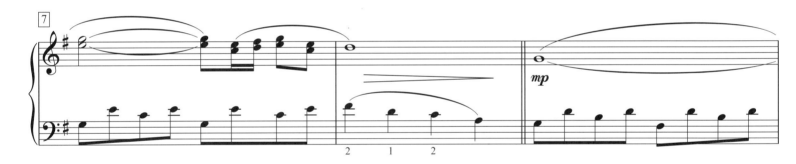

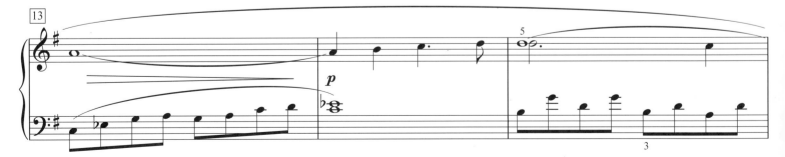

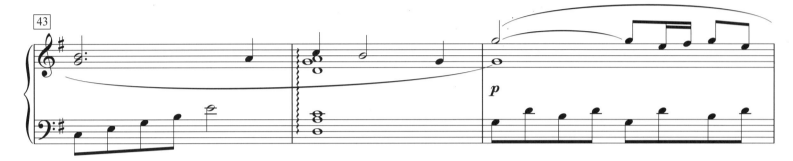

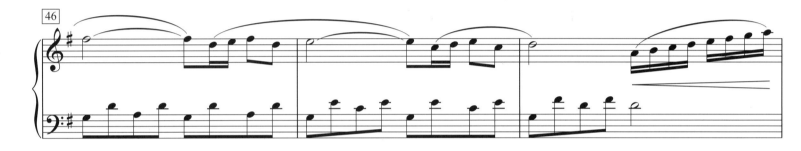

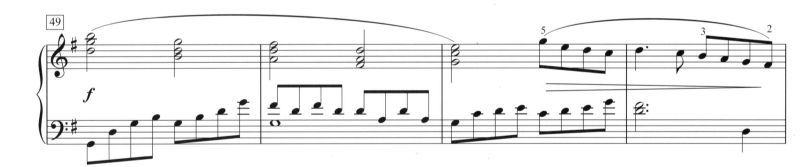

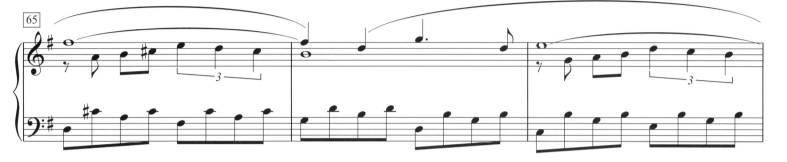

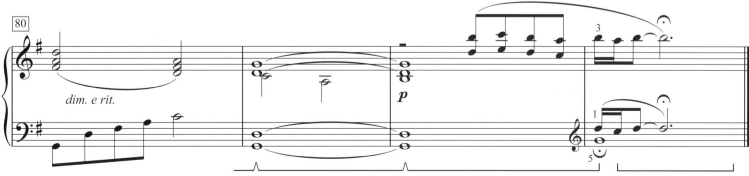

GOODBYE TO LOVE

Words and Music by RICHARD CARPENTER
and JOHN BETTIS
Arranged by Phillip Keveren

Expressive Ballad ♩ = c. 76

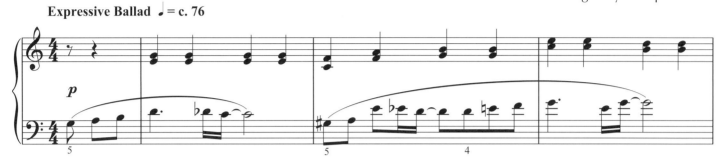

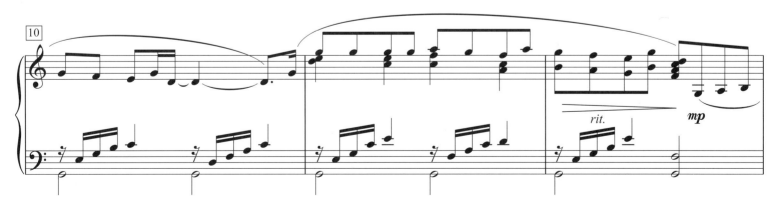

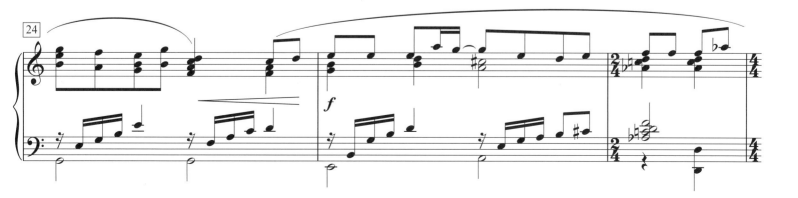

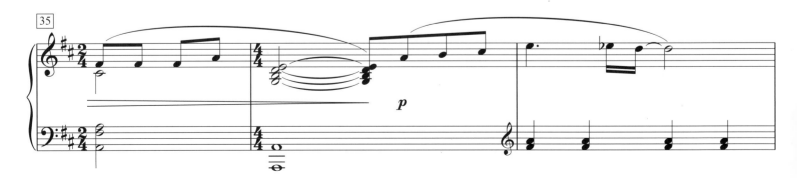

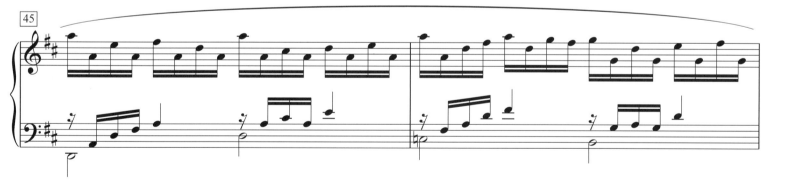

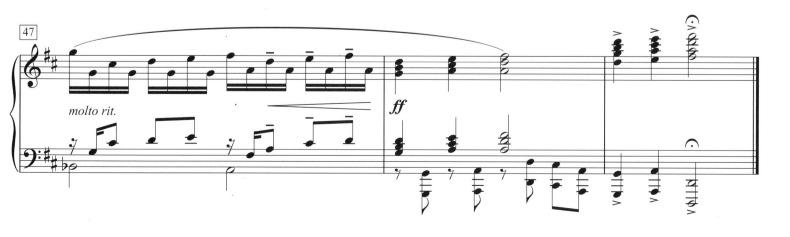

HURTING EACH OTHER

Words by PETER UDELL
Music by GARY GELD
Arranged by Phillip Keveren

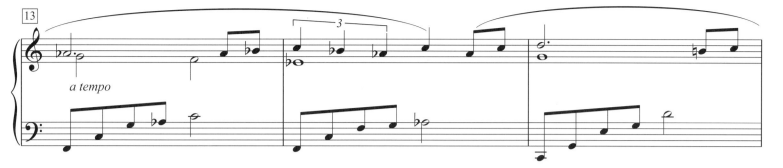

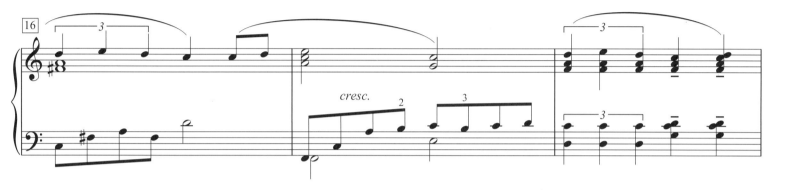

(R.H. over L.H.)

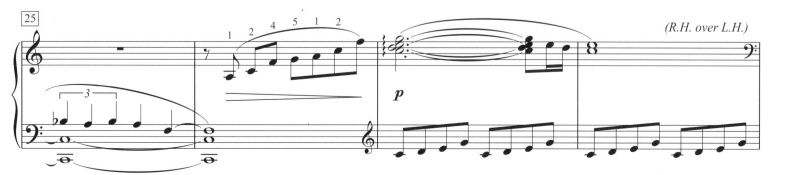

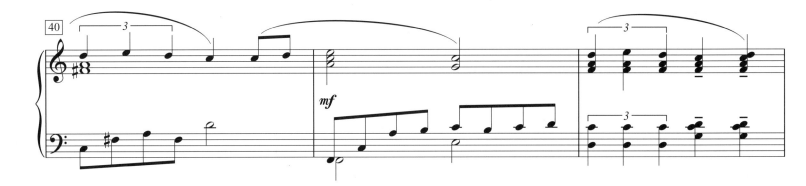

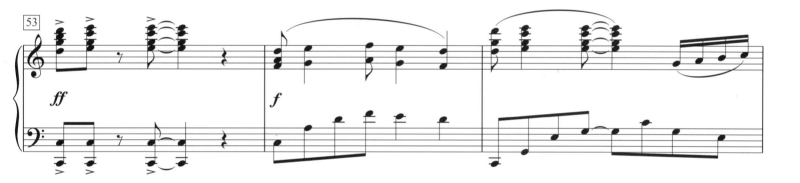

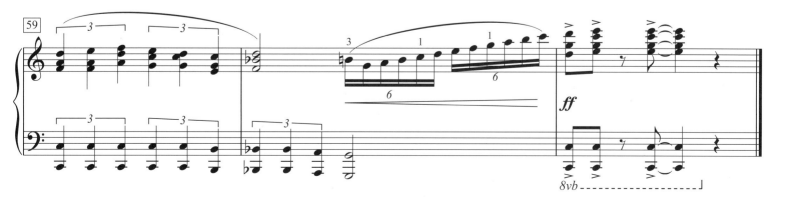

I NEED TO BE IN LOVE

Words and Music by RICHARD CARPENTER,
JOHN BETTIS and ALBERT HAMMOND
Arranged by Phillip Keveren

Cantabile ♩ = c. 72

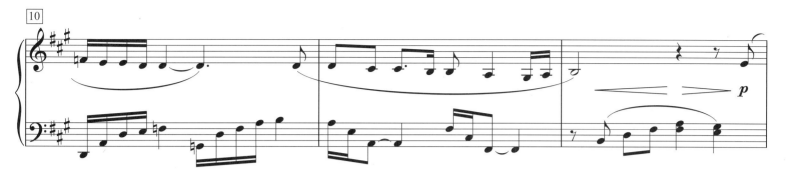

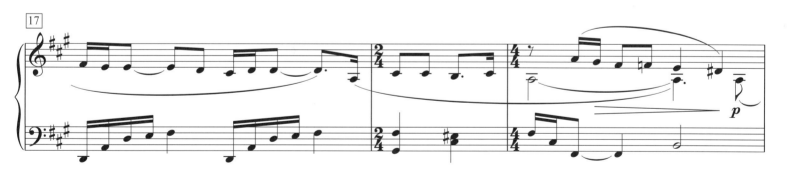

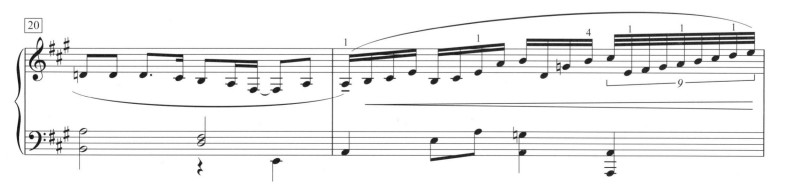

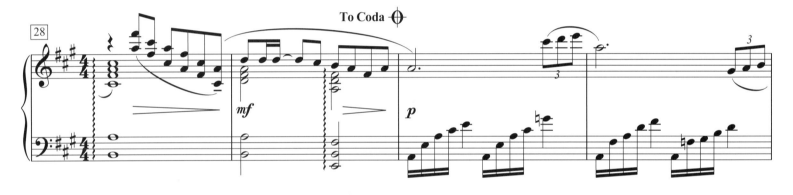

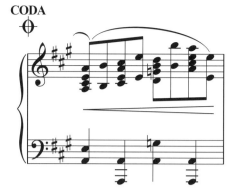

I WON'T LAST A DAY WITHOUT YOU

Words and Music by PAUL WILLIAMS
and ROGER NICHOLS
Arranged by Phillip Keveren

Gently, with rubato ♩ = c. 72

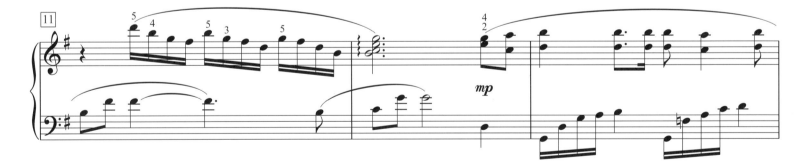

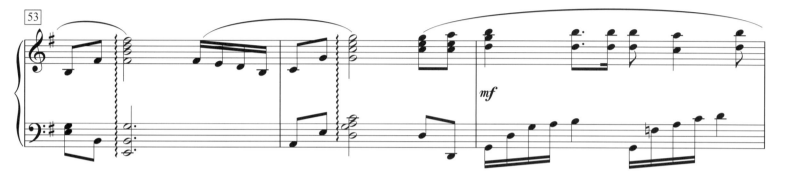

IT'S GOING TO TAKE SOME TIME

Words and Music by CAROLE KING
and TONI STERN
Arranged by Phillip Keveren

Steady ♩ = 116

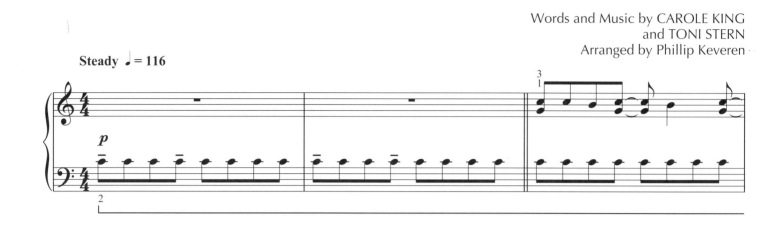

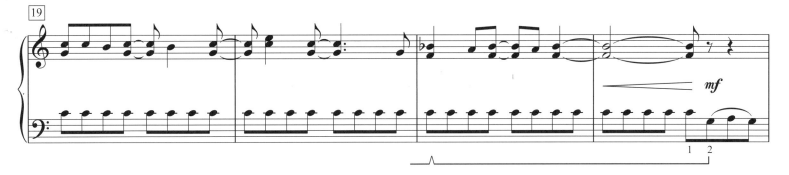

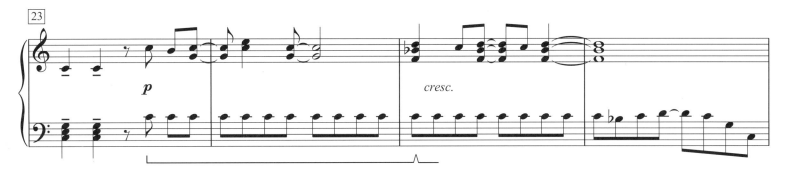

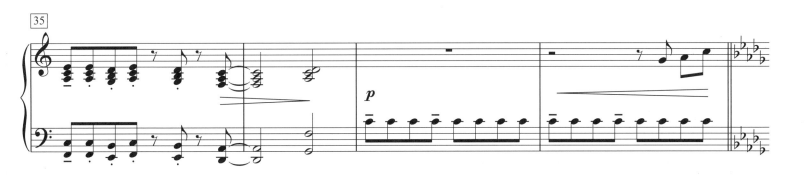

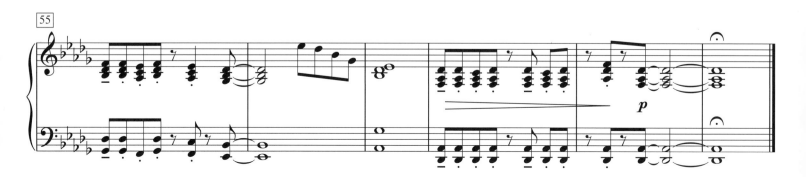

MR. GUDER

Words and Music by JOHN BETTIS
and RICHARD CARPENTER
Arranged by Phillip Keveren

With a classical flair ♩ = 152–160

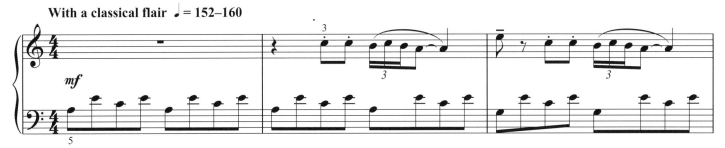

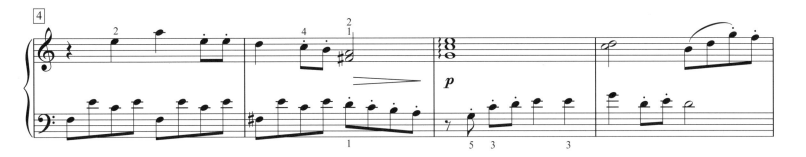

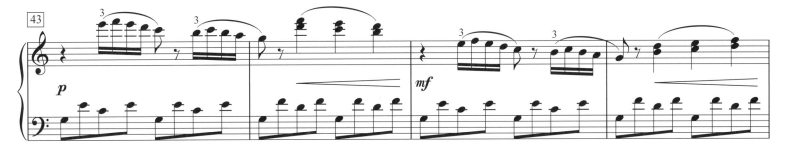

PLEASE MR. POSTMAN

Words and Music by ROBERT BATEMAN,
GEORGIA DOBBINS, WILLIAM GARRETT,
FREDDIE GORMAN and BRIAN HOLLAND
Arranged by Phillip Keveren

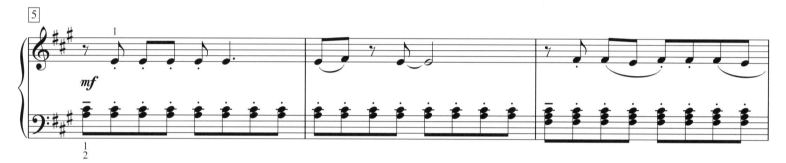

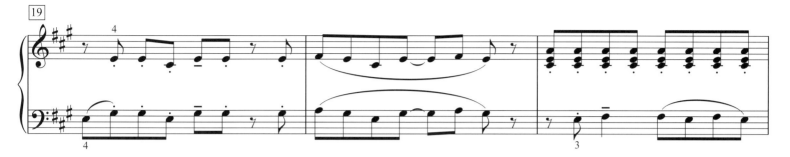

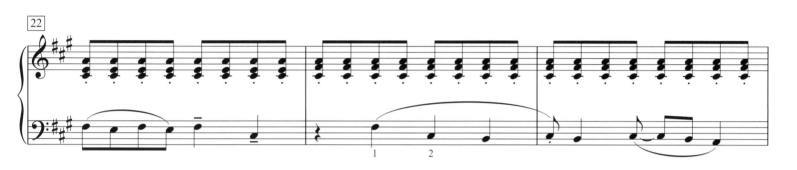

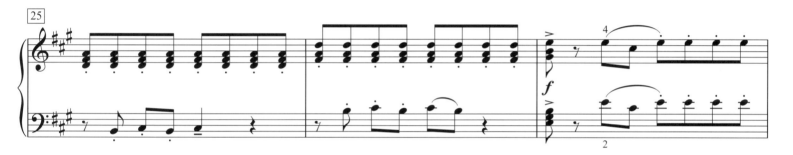

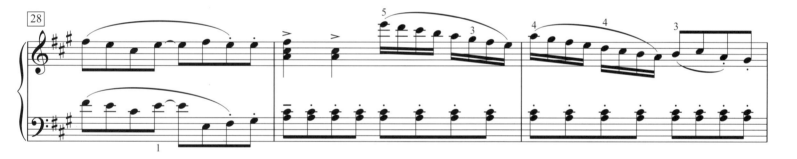

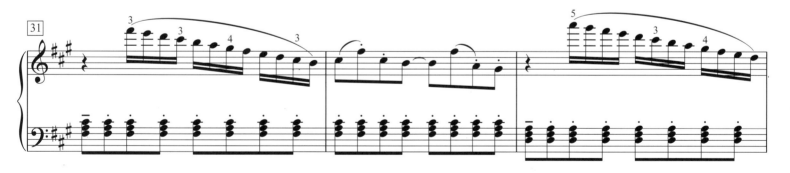

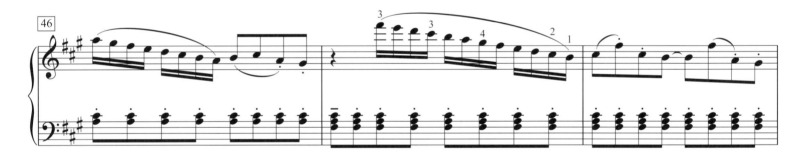

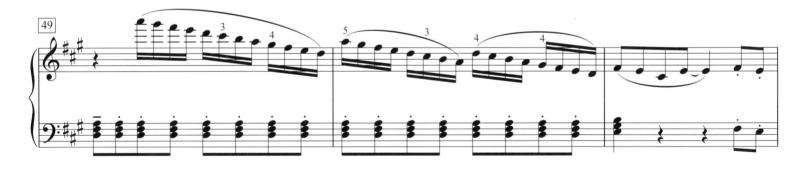

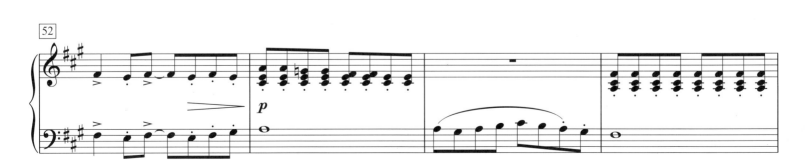

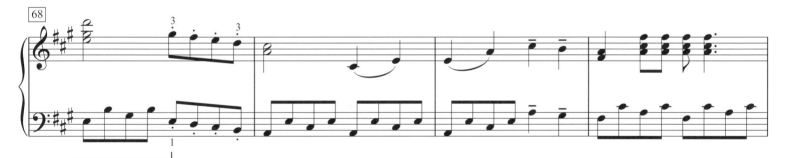

RAINY DAYS AND MONDAYS

Lyrics by PAUL WILLIAMS
Music by ROGER NICHOLS
Arranged by Phillip Keveren

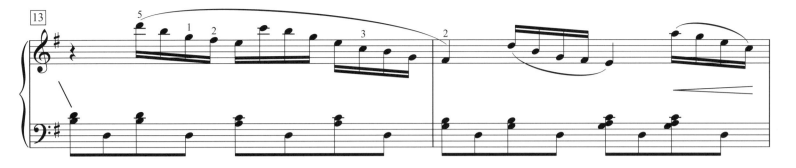

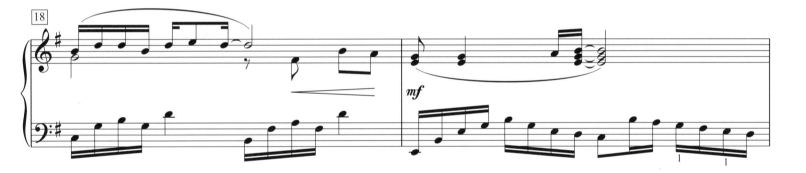

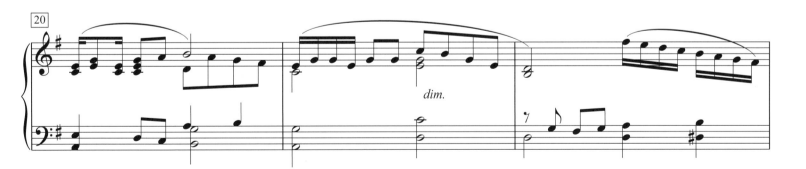

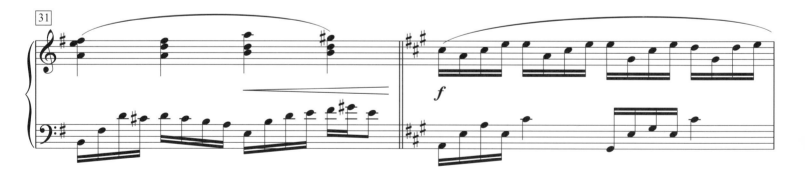

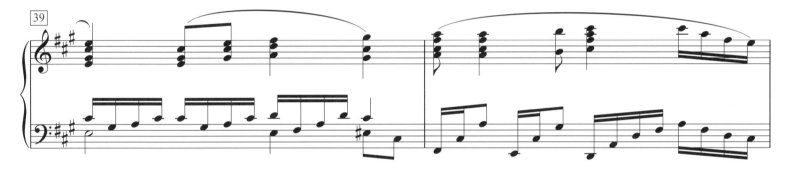

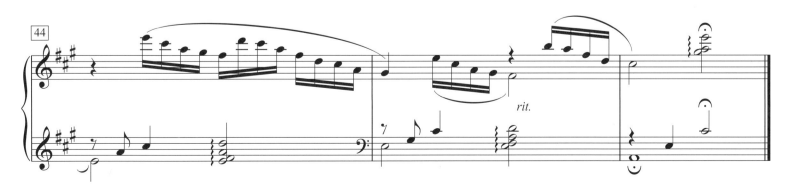

SING
from SESAME STREET

Words and Music by JOE RAPOSO
Arranged by Phillip Keveren

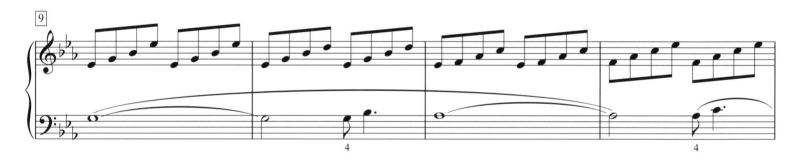

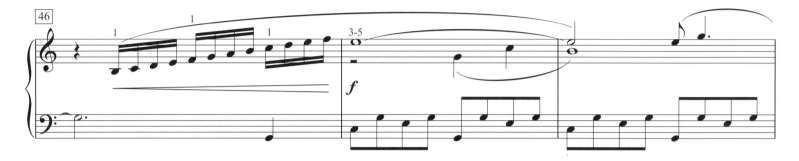

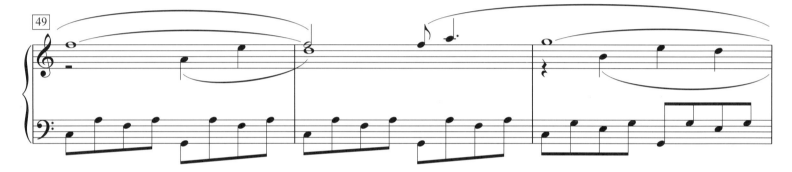

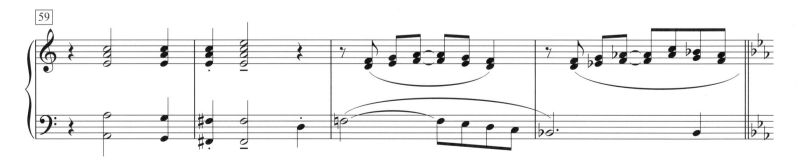

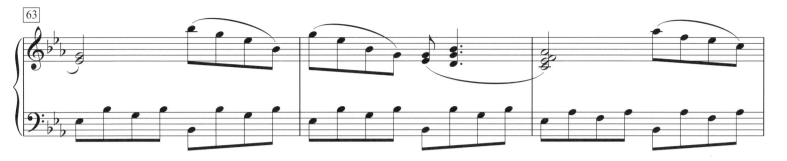

SOLITAIRE

Words and Music by NEIL SEDAKA
and PHIL CODY
Arranged by Phillip Keveren

Expressively, with rubato ♩ = c. 66

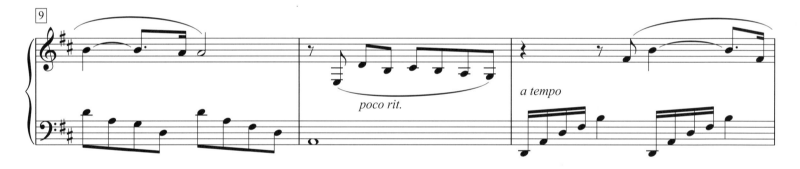

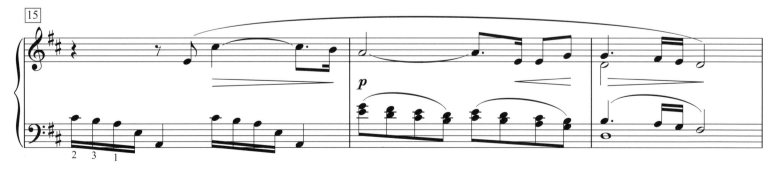

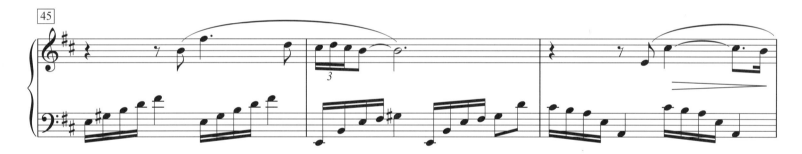

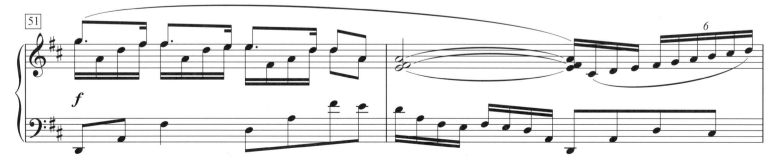

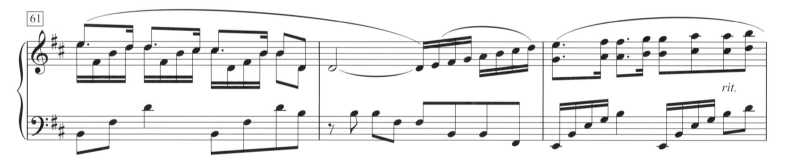

SUPERSTAR

Words and Music by LEON RUSSELL
and BONNIE SHERIDAN
Arranged by Phillip Keveren

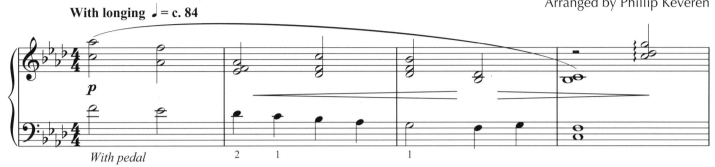

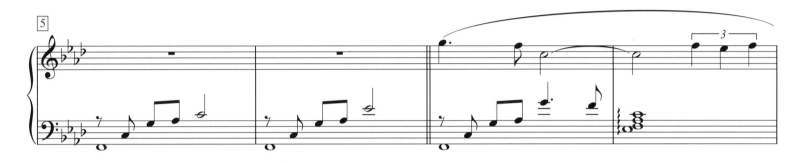

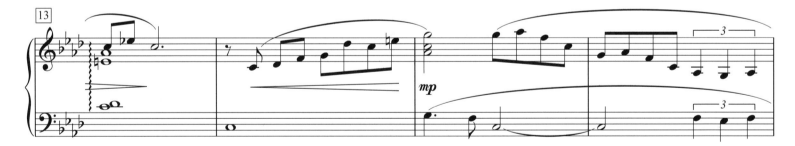

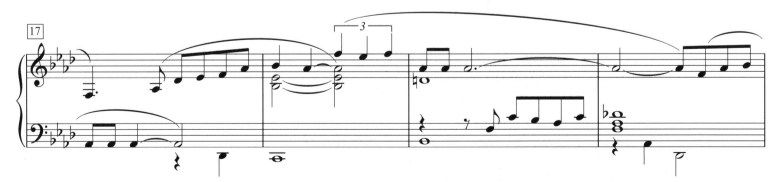

Assertively ♩ = c. 60

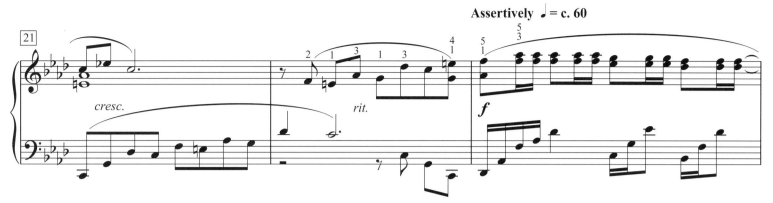

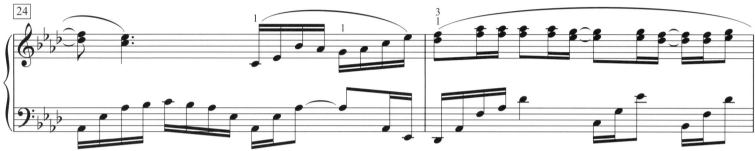

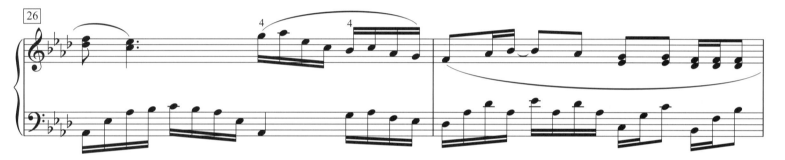

Tempo I ♩ = c. 84

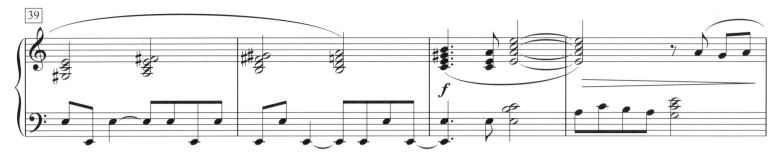

THIS MASQUERADE

Words and Music by LEON RUSSELL
Arranged by Phillip Keveren

TICKET TO RIDE

Words and Music by JOHN LENNON
and PAUL McCARTNEY
Arranged by Phillip Keveren

Flowing ♩ = c. 92

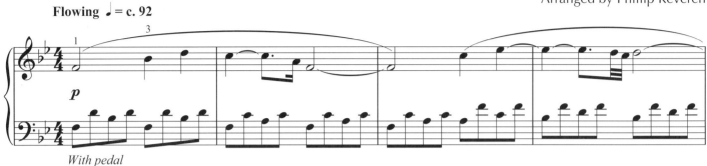

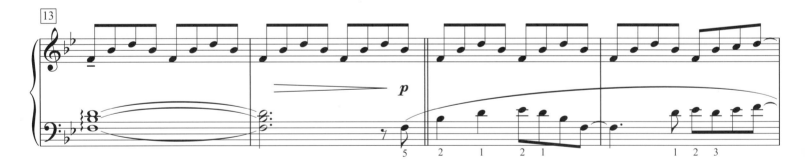

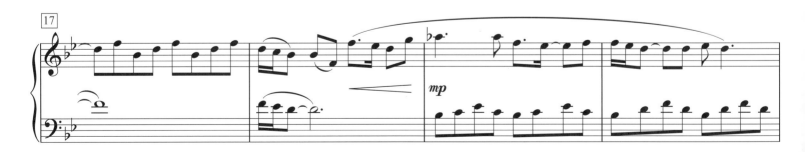

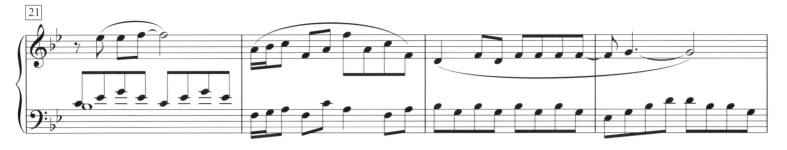

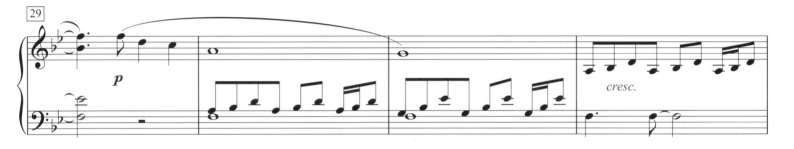

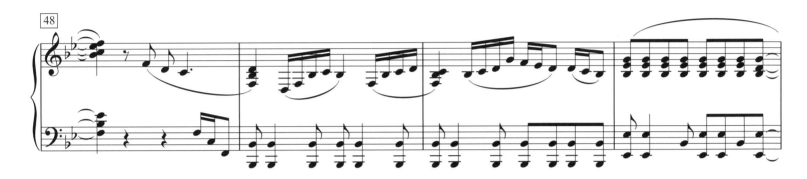

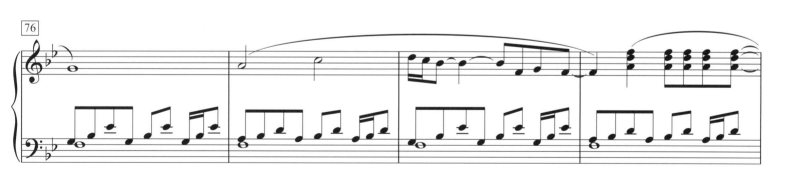

TOP OF THE WORLD

Words and Music by JOHN BETTIS
and RICHARD CARPENTER
Arranged by Phillip Keveren

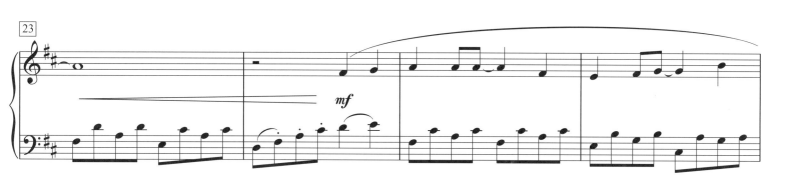

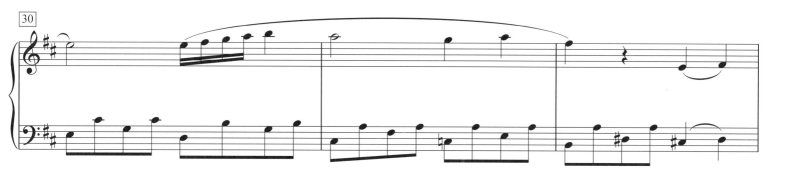

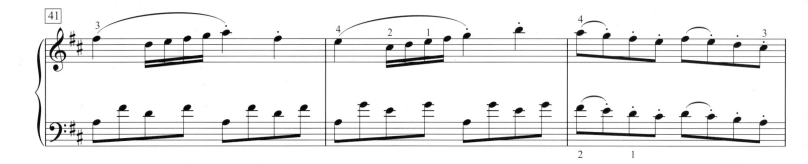

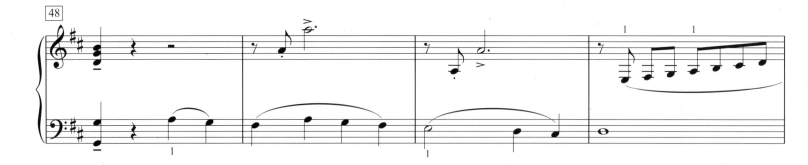

WE'VE ONLY JUST BEGUN

Words and Music by ROGER NICHOLS
and PAUL WILLIAMS
Arranged by Phillip Keveren

Moderately slow ♩ = 84–88

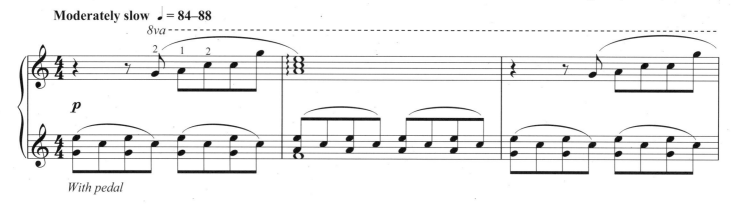

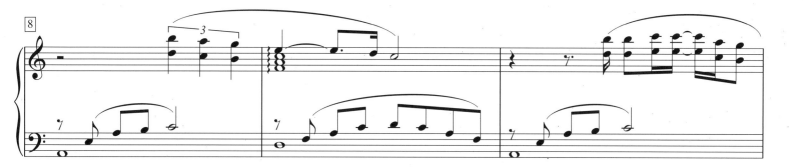

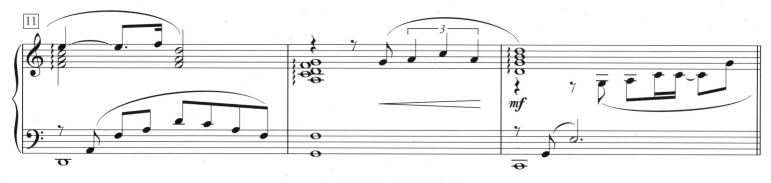

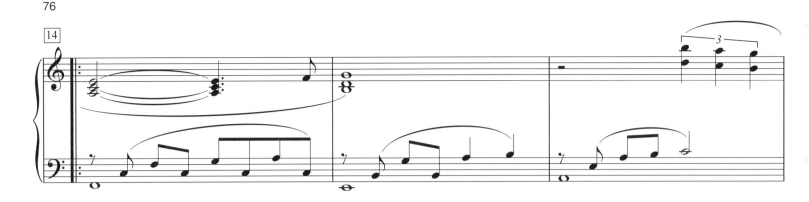

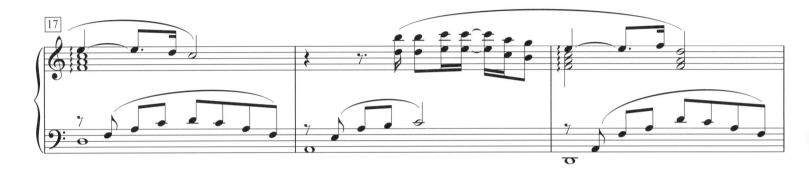

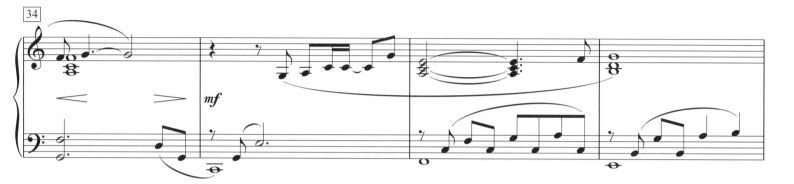

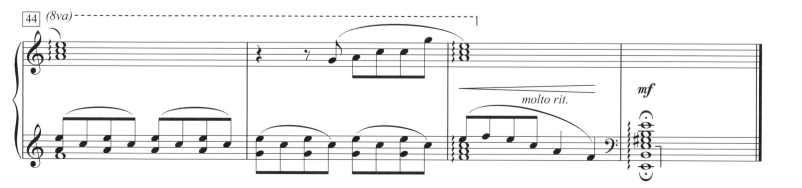

YESTERDAY ONCE MORE

Words and Music by JOHN BETTIS
and RICHARD CARPENTER
Arranged by Phillip Keveren